The Country
DECORATIVE PAINTING
Companion

The Country
DECORATIVE PAINTING
Companion

Judith and Martin Miller

PHOTOGRAPHY BY JAMES MERRELL

CollinsPublishersSanFrancisco

A Division of HarperCollins*Publishers*

The Country Decorative Painting Companion
Judith and Martin Miller

First published in USA in 1995
by Collins Publishers San Francisco
1160 Battery Street, San Francisco CA 94111

First published in Great Britain in 1995 by Mitchell Beazley
an imprint of Reed Consumer Books Limited

Photography by *James Merrell*
Photographs on pages 30, 31, 54 & 55 by *Andrew Twort*
Illustrations by *Michael Hill*

Art Editor	*Peta Waddington*
Editors	*Sophie Pearse and Jonathan Hilton*
Art Director	*Jacqui Small*
Executive Editor	*Judith More*
Production	*Heather O'Connell*

Library of Congress Cataloging-in-Publication Data
Miller, Judith
    The country decorative painting companion/Judith and Martin Miller: photography by James Merrell.
      p.   cm.
    ISBN 0-00-255490-9
    1. Painting. 2. Decoration and ornament. I. Miller, Martin.
II. Title.
TT385.M53 1995
698'.3--dc20   94-24446
                                                        CIP

The publishers have made every effort to ensure that all instructions given in this book are accurate and safe,
but they cannot accept liability for any resulting injury, damage or loss to either person or property, whether
direct or consequential and howsoever arising. The authors and publishers will be grateful for any information
which will assist them in keeping future editions up to date.

Colour reproduction by Rival Colour, UK
Produced by Mandarin Offset
Printed and bound in China

INTRODUCTION

The variety of decorative paint and other types of color finishes and effects that have been used in homes throughout the ages is enormous. Many of these, such as woodgraining, started out in the homes of the wealthy townsfolk and were subsequently copied by itinerant artists who traveled the countryside plying their trade.

Other finishes and effects, such as limewash and stenciling, have always had a place in humbler homes as inexpensive methods of decoration. Limewash is one of the first paints to have been devised and it has been used to decorate all manner of homes for thousands of years. It is still used in some traditionally built country homes to this day as a method of preserving not only the appearance but also the fabric of these buildings. The chalky, powdery look characteristic of a limewash finish is so appealing that many decorators emulate it in the more easily available contemporary paints that are now produced.

Limewash and other traditional formulations for paints can still be found through specialist suppliers. However, for safety reasons many of these traditional paints have to be handled with care and therefore they are generally used only by professionals.

Some companies produce paints that copy the look of the original versions but are formulated with safer, modern ingredients intended for amateurs to use. You can obtain milk paint, for example, with all the opacity and the authentic rich color range of the original but without the harmful lead or lime content.

As well as using special paint formulations, there are other ways to impose a period feel by creating an antique look on a new surface. For example, painted metal can be treated to give it a well-worn, aged appearance. And raw, newly painted joinery can be aged so that it blends in with a period scheme, while bright, fresh paintwork on furniture can be distressed to give it an impression of age and general wear and tear.

Opposite Left: *Modern, soft green paint with a traditional feel is true to the spirit of authentic 18th-century wood paneling.* **Opposite Right**: *A coat of green paint gives a chair visual impact against a contrasting colored wall.* **Above**: *A simple leaf motif stencil is used to decorate a wall.*

COLORS

CHOOSING COLORS

The very first colors known to our prehistoric ancestors would have been made from locally occurring organic and inorganic materials. These would have included plant extracts, colored earths, and crushed minerals, mixed with water or any other conveniently available source of liquid such as saliva.

Above: *Scandinavian colorwashed walls.* **Below**: *A Spanish house with brilliant white walls.*

The modern paint industry today still uses – although by no means exclusively – some of these same types of naturally occurring colorant. However, since the introduction of the first chemical pigments in the 19th century, our choice of color for walls and furniture has become immeasurably wider and the effects more stable.

Above: *Cool blue colorwashed walls.* **Below:** *A pale wall color picks up reflected hues.*

The desire to add pattern and color to our home environment is a continuous thread that runs through mankind's history. Although our modern perception is that medieval homes were rather dimly lit, somber colored, and largely monochromatic, they were in fact often painted in a rich variety of hues.

This polychromatic fashion lasted up until the 17th century. However, it was not until about 1750 that light schemes took hold in the English-speaking world and in Holland and Germany. During the 18th century, these French-influenced pale colors had also reached Scandinavia. By the mid 18th century in England, flat color was being used as a foil to rich decorative techniques such as graining, marbling, and gilding. During the same period in North America, the Colonial palette combined earth

13

colors, such as almond, red, and brown, with very bright blues, greens, and yellows. And the later Federal taste included shades of terra cotta and deep pinks, along with stone colors and also gray. Although 18th-century colors could be very vivid, the composition of paints available at that time was quite unstable and so the strength of colors waned very rapidly once exposed to the air. The invention of aniline dyes in the mid 19th century created a fashion for sharp yellows, intense blues, and acid greens of a chemical intensity unknown previously. Even when earthy reds or browns were used, they tended to be brightened with gold or yellows.

Below left: *Terra cotta and deep green create a rich contrast in the stairway of this 18th-century French house.* **Below right**: *Throughout the Mediterranean region, intense blue is a recurring color theme.* **Opposite**: *Vivid blue-green gives a South American ambience to an 18th-century Maine farmhouse.*

LIMEWASHING

As a protective and decorative finish for plaster, render, masonry, and, to a lesser extent, wood, limewash was in common use for thousands of years prior to the middle of the 19th century. Although the use of limewash declined with the advent of modern building materials and synthetic paints, it remains aesthetically desirable and an essential protective finish for many buildings made of traditional materials.

While the constituents have varied slightly, the basic wash is made by slaking lump lime in water to produce lime putty. This putty is then mixed with water and a water-proofing agent, such as animal fat, to produce a milk-like wash. If several untinted coats are applied, the wash dries to a "pure" white that changes subtly in appearance depending on the light and weather conditions. For example, it can appear as a dazzling, luminous white, which is best associated with the vernacular architecture of the Mediterranean, or take on a darker, matte, chalky appearance when wet or when seen under overcast conditions, such as those that often prevail in northern Europe.

As an alternative to the basic whitewash, pigments can be added – usually earth colors and by-products of the mining industry, such as iron and chrome oxide, cobalt, copper carbonate, and cadmium.

Apart from being aesthetically pleasing, limewash's most important

Above left & right: *An example of pastel and earth-colored limewash.* **Below left:** *A pale ocher limewash tones with warm-colored floor tiles.* **Below right:** *Country furniture set against colored limewashed surfaces.*

characteristic is that it allows the underlying surface to "breathe". Country homes made of traditional materials, such as wattle and daub and cob, and lime renders and plasters, absorb moisture from their surroundings and rapidly decay if they become saturated. Limewash helps to lessen

Right: The authentic appearance of old limewashed walls cannot be matched by modern, synthetic paints. **Opposite & below:** *This cob house has limewashed walls to protect it against decay.*

the absorption of moisture and also allows the evaporation of any moisture that is already in the substrate.

Due to the caustic nature of slaked lime, limewash also has important disinfectant properties. On paneling and unpainted furniture, limewash was used to deter woodworm and other insect infestations. Although most often associated with farm houses and cottages, limewash was also used on civic and religious buildings and on grander domestic dwellings.

MILK PAINT

Prior to the end of the 19th century, premixed pigments and paints were rarely available outside of cities and large towns. In North America, Europe, and Scandinavia itinerant painters who traveled between towns and villages had to mix paints and glazes on site, and augment the limited range of materials they carried with them with locally available ingredients. For many painters, milk paint (buttermilk or casein paint) offered an excellent opportunity due to its readily available, affordable ingredients, ease of preparation and application, durability, and strength of color.

Milk paint was made by mixing earth-colored pigments with buttermilk or skimmed milk and a little lime (for its insecticidal and fungicidal properties). It was particularly popular in North America during the late 18th and 19th centuries. Milk paint dries to a smooth, flat finish and has a clarity of color that is not often found in modern, synthetic paints.

Left: *Soft milk paints have a beauty rarely achieved by ready-mixed paints.* **Opposite**: *Milk paint matched to the original 18th-century hue.*

PAINT
EFFECTS

Above: *Printed stenciled wallpaper, copied from original 18th- and 19th-century designs. During the 18th and much of the 19th centuries, stenciling was an inexpensive alternative to costly hand-printed wallpapers.* **Opposite**: *The stenciled bedroom in the American Museum in Bath, England.*

STENCILING

Stenciling is a method of transferring a motif or pattern onto a contrasting colored background by applying paint through cut-outs in a stencil sheet. There is evidence that stenciling was used in very early cultures. The Chinese, for example, are credited with having developed the art of stenciling in about 3000 BC, with stencil-printed artifacts, such as silks and papers, having been discovered at Tunhuang in west China. There are also many surviving examples of Egyptian stenciled artefacts, most notably repeat designs on some mummy cases. Today, most stencil patterns are cut from either oil-card or sheets of clear acetate; but in cultures that are less technological, however, there is a tendency to use whatever materials there are to hand, such as the Inuit people's use of dried seal skins, or banana and bamboo leaves that are employed by the Fijian Islanders.

In medieval Britain, stenciling was largely confined to church interiors, where walls were embellished with traditional heraldic motifs in red-, green-, and gold-colored pigments. Although faded, some of these motifs have survived, and many of them later

reappeared in the Gothic Revivalists' designs for wallpaper and tiles. In 15th-century England, stenciled wall-hangings of burlap were to be found in grander dwellings, and unpaneled, limewashed walls provided a most suitable background for hand-painted or stenciled patterns.

In France, stenciling was popular as early as the Middle Ages and was used on textiles and books as well as for interior decoration. By the 14th century, the French had developed a method for producing hand-blocked wall-hangings, a process that involved applying chopped wool onto sheets of hand-made paper previously impressed and stenciled with rabbit glue. Due to the effects of damp and rodent

Right: *A simple leaf motif stenciled on the walls acts as a backdrop for a fine collection of provincial furniture and 19th-century pottery. A traditional green milk paint gives it a time-worn appearance.*

infestation that were common in the average home at that time, few examples have survived to the present day. Fortunately, however, some 16th-century French papers, printed with small, geometric motifs – mostly black – and then hand stenciled and applied to pieces of furniture, have withstood the test of time.

With the introduction of exquisite hand-painted wallpapers in Europe, particularly in France and England, at the end of the 17th century and throughout the 18th century, hand stenciling became less fashionable as a means of decorating entire walls in the homes of the wealthy. However, in Britain during the second half of the 18th century, it was common to see walls painted in plain, flat colors augmented with borders – often simple Greek or Egyptian motifs – applied freehand or stenciled. Later, a feature

Above: *A repeat-pattern frieze on wooden planks.*
Opposite: *Stenciled wallpaper from an original design.* **Below:** *A flower-and-leaf stenciled motif.*

Above: *Furniture can be decorated with stencils. A paint-on resist and a stencil created the design on this stained chest.* **Opposite:** *Small areas of stenciling give new life to a simple wooden pine desk.*

While the ever-increasing availability of wallpapers during the 18th and 19th centuries had the effect of making hand-stenciled decorations either less desirable or, compared with the mass-produced printed papers now coming onto the market, less affordable to many city dwellers, in rural areas it was a very different story. In the country-side, wallpapers and silks were usually too expensive, often unsuitable for hanging on the commonly damp wooden or plaster walls, or, particularly in the case of the North American colonies, simply not readily available.

In these North American communities, stenciling was transformed into a form of folk art, and it represented a relatively inexpensive way of introducing color and pattern into the home and, at the same time, imitating the wallpapered interiors of the wealthier town and city households.

of the splendors of late 19th-century decorations was the embellishment of ceilings, especially in the main reception rooms, with stenciled garlands of flowers and fruit in rich colors.

PAINTED FURNITURE

The modern trend toward stripping wooden artifacts of their original painted finish – especially pine furniture – has, unfortunately, done much to destroy an important strand of the history of traditional country furniture throughout the world.

Although often primitive in its construction, county-style furniture did not eschew decoration or ornamentation. Our forebears discovered that one of the easiest ways of adding a touch of brightness to the often austere interiors of their isolated cottages or farmhouses was to apply coats of whitewash or limewash and, later, milk paint – which could all be easily

Above: A Swedish wooden wall cupboard dating from about 1790 with traces of its original paintwork visible. **Opposite:** *Multicolored walls and furniture in a late-19th-century Texan house.*

made from ingredients readily to hand. A later development was oil-based paint, which used linseed oil as the carrier medium for the colorants. And not only flat colors were used – there is still much evidence of a rich tradition

of pattern and design in painted furniture from North and South America, Asia, Europe, and Scandinavia.

However, it would be incorrect to think that painted furniture was restricted solely to the homes of the country poor. Wealthy urbanites in the 17th century, for example, spared no expense in employing expert artists to simulate realistically painted wood-grain effects on furniture and joinery.

As fashions changed over the years, so did the color and pattern applied to items of furniture. By carefully removing the layers of paintwork built up over the centuries, you will soon discover what hue or style was fashionable at different periods in history. And if you have restoration in mind, then look at examples of period pieces that have escaped the heat gun and chemical stripper. You will find that many of the colors are not really too

difficult to emulate with modern paint formulations, some of which are based on age-old traditional recipes.

Apply different colored coats of paint patchily onto the bare wood, then apply an even top coat. Rub the paint with damp wet-and-dry paper to reveal the underlying color and grain.

Opposite: *A painted paneled cupboard typical of the Tyrolean peasant tradition.* **Below:** *Europe has always been a melting pot of different styles, here Tyrolean and mid-European traditions.*

BROKEN COLOR

Many period finishes and effects are created by using techniques that have their origins in fine art. These are now known as broken color techniques – that is, methods of distressing a semi-translucent paint or glaze, applied over a contrasting-colored, opaque groundcoat, to produce patterns and subtle gradations of color over a surface. The effects can be aesthetically pleasing in their own right, a replication of a natural material, such as wood or marble, or a simulation of a naturally occurring chemical process, such as the breakdown of pigments commonly found in many traditional paints.

Colorwashing involves applying thin washes of glaze over a groundcoat in order to build up subtle veils of color over a surface. Brush marks are usually retained to give additional pattern, texture, and body.

Ragging is a process of brushing out a glaze over an opaque groundcoat and then dabbing it with a loosely bunched rag, moistened with solvent, to remove patches of glaze. The result is an attractively random pattern that

simulates the traditional flat-painted surfaces that have become mottled due to the breakdown of pigment.

Sponging involves dabbing a sponge, moistened with solvent, over a water- or oil-based glaze to create a random, speckled pattern.

Combing is a technique that involves dragging a comb, cut from oiled-card, plastic or steel, through a wet glaze to produce a series of vertical, horizontal, or wavy stripes that allow the groundcoat to "ghost" through. Combing is used to simulate figuring in fantasy woodgrains.

Dragging effects are produced by pulling the bristles of a special dragging brush down through a wet glaze in a series of parallel motions to form a uniformly striped finish that simulates woodgrain.

Stippling involves tapping the bristle tips of a stippling brush over a

Above: *14th-century colorwashed walls in ocher and Indian red.* Opposite: *This sponged wall was given two red and one off-white oil-based glazes.*

wet glaze to blend different glazes together to create subtle shadings and gradations of color.

Spattering is produced by flicking flecks of wet glaze randomly over an opaque groundcoat, creating an overlay of colored specks. Spattering is sometimes done to simulate insect infestation in painted joinery.

COLORWASHING

Distemper was the traditional ingredient used in colorwashing applied to walls. However, for better coverage and durability, but without sacrificing any authenticity, there are ways you can use modern paint formulations.

After preparing and priming the wall to be colorwashed, apply one or two coats of your base paint – a standard, modern eggshell-finish paint or one you have personalized by the addition of other colors. Use a large decorator's brush for this. When the base color is dry, make up a glaze consisting of a toning color of eggshell paint, and a transparent oil glaze (the medium) mixed with mineral spirits (white spirits) in the ratio of 3:1. Mix 1 part of the paint with every 12 parts of the medium. Again using a large decorator's brush, apply the glaze roughly to the wall. Brush the glaze in all directions, making no attempt to disguise brush marks so that the base color "ghosts" through.

Left and opposite: *Colorwashed walls lend a sense of harmony to furniture spanning different centuries in this medieval house, in Avon, England, dating back to the reign of Edward III.*

MARBLING

Decorative painters were employed to simulate the appearance of marble principally because the cost of quarrying, cutting, and polishing the stone made it expensive, and transportation costs from the quarries, mainly in Italy and France, were very high. However, even when cost was not a factor, marble was still sometimes simulated because the real stone was not suitable for certain types of building construction.

Sophisticated marbling began on a large scale in Italy and France during the Renaissance. The fine examples that adorned many important civic and residential buildings established a tradition of precise, formal, and flamboyant marbling that has survived in both countries up to the present day.

In 17th-century England, the sumptuous interiors of many palaces and large houses featured imaginative, if rather crudely executed, marbled paneling, plasterwork, columns, and joinery, reflecting the Italian influence. The standard of marbling improved over the centuries, and by the 19th century examples can be found that are almost indistinguishable from the real thing. Many fine examples of realistic marbling can also be seen throughout Scandinavia. However, in the regional tradition of naive ("farmer") marbling, the effects are crude and tend to run riot over every conceivable surface.

Opposite: A rare 18th-century Swedish painted cupboard showing a marbled decoration in the naive "farmer" tradition. The effect is abstract and is not meant to emulate the real stone.

AGEING
EFFECTS

AGEING PAINT

After exposure to sunlight and damp, dust and dirt, central heating and air conditioning, as well as the general wear and tear of generations of use and misuse, painted period furniture, walls, frames and general joinery, and metalwork almost inevitably displays some of the signs of ageing.

Once pristine, paintwork will fade, darken, flake, chip, or craze depending on the conditions under which it has been kept and the degree to which it has been cared for. Rather than necessarily being a problem, the patination of age may be aesthetically pleasing, and could even add to the value of a piece of period furniture. For example, much of the real worth – both financial and historic – of much painted furniture, old metal chests and metal food cupboards, doors and dadoes, and similar painted

Opposite: *A combination of Mexican and Native American styles is leant authenticity by faded and aged paintwork.* Left: *The paintwork on this Pennsylvania pie cupboard dates back to 1790.* Right: *Paintwork on an old armoire is chipped and flaked around the areas of most wear and tear.*

items was obliterated in an orgy of wood and metal stripping during the two decades of the 1960s and 70s.

Modern homemakers are today – perhaps with some insight into the mistakes of their youthful enthusiasm

Below: *19th-century paint revealed when the plank walls were rubbed back.* **Opposite**: *Rubbed brown paint reveals traces of a contrasting basecoat.*

– once more learning to appreciate the esthetic appeal of painted effects, but are now faced with the problem of making paint look genuinely mellow and old. The wheel has indeed turned full circle.

One of the simpler methods of ageing paint is to apply an oil-based antiquing glaze consisting of, for example, artists' oils, such as burnt umber, Vandyke brown, and black, suspended in a clear medium of transparent oil glaze (scumble) and mineral spirits (white spirit). The glaze darkens the surface of the paint, simulating the dirt and grime that naturally becomes embedded in the surface over a period of years. To increase the "authenticity" of the effect, apply greater concentrations of the glaze to the recesses of moldings and other areas where you would normally expect dirt and grime to accumulate through constant use.

PAINTED WOOD

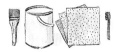

Due to exposure to general atmospheric conditions and everyday wear and tear, painted wooden surfaces will, in time, begin to exhibit various signs of ageing. For example, if the pigments on an area of wall paneling or on a piece of painted furniture or on a box or tray are exposed to bright sunlight, their color will naturally lighten due to a bleaching process. Conversely, an accumulation of dirt, dust, and grime on a wooden surface will tend to darken the original color of the paint.

Exposure to heat, too, may also take its toll – the expansion and contraction of the wood as it heats up and cools down causes the paint to crack and lift off the base wood beneath. Damage such as this is all part of the natural ageing process, but new pieces of painted wood can be given an antique appearance by simulating some of these "problems".

One of the easiest method of ageing paintwork is to rub it down with

Opposite: *The wallpaper has been stripped to reveal 18th-century paint.* **Below**: *Original blue-green paneling hidden under five coats of paint.*

an abrasive material. If gently done, the action of the abrasive will lighten the color of the paint and simulate the effects of exposure to sunlight. Heavy rubbing back may expose underlying coats of paint and this could simulate the effects of heavy wear and tear and give the impression of greater age.

Painted wooden surfaces also sometimes tend to craze over time. One way of simulating this look involves applying two coats of a pro-

prietary *craquelure* (crackle) varnish over the painted surface. Apply the second coat about one hour after the first – or when the first coat is just tacky. Because the first coat has started to dry, and therefore is contracting at a faster rate than the second one, it pulls the second coat apart, causing fine cracks and crazing.

Painted wooden surfaces exposed to damp over a period of time may start to flake. You can simulate this particular effect by rubbing patches of bare, unpainted woodwork with beeswax. After painting, gently rub back the areas you have waxed with an abrasive material and the paint should immediately start to flake off.

Left: *Old pieces of wooden furniture may be truer to their original appearance if surviving paintwork is left intact.* **Opposite**: *A beautifully aged painted Mexican cupboard relies for its decorative effect on the thinnest washes of paint.*

LIMING

In 16th-century Europe, furniture and paneling made from open-grain woods such as oak and ash, and pale-colored woods such as pine and elm, were often treated with a caustic lime paste in order to lighten or "bleach" the wood and protect it against insect infestations. The subtle effect produced by the white pigment left behind in the grain of the wood was much admired and, by the 17th century, liming furniture and joinery had become a fashionable decorative technique. Today, proprietary liming pastes and waxes are readily available, but a far simpler and less time-consuming technique using paint can be employed as a substitute.

Starting with new wood, or wood that has been stripped and allowed to dry, rub the surface with a wire brush to open the grain. Apply a coat of unthinned white latex (matte emulsion). Then, before the paint has dried, wipe off all excess paint using a pad made up of clean, lint-free rag.

Left: *Attractive, lime-bleached floorboards are particularly associated with Scandinavian-style period interiors.* *Opposite*: *An 18th-century Welsh press whitewashed to gave a limed effect.*

AGEING METAL

If exposed to the effects of the atmosphere, the surface of artifacts and architectural fixtures and fittings made of metals, such as bronze, copper, brass, steel, and lead – but not stainless steel – are naturally prone to ageing and deterioration. The chemical reactions that take place gradually over the years produce a patination on the surface of the metal that can not only be visually pleasing, but will also lend the object in question a distinctive air of antiquity.

The value of genuinely old metal objects can be seriously reduced if the patination is removed or damaged through over-zealous cleaning.

The decorative appeal of naturally patinated metal is such that painters and craftsmen have devised a variety of methods of antiquing new metal

surfaces and objects using different paint techniques. For example, you can simulate the effects of verdigris – a green and white crumbly paste that builds up on the surface of bronze, copper, and brass – by using a combination of paints, glazes, and powders. An ordinary metal watering can, wire hanging basket, or the type of metal patio chair or table you might find outside in any garden, can be quite believably transformed into an "antique" and attractive garden or conservatory ornament that appears to be heavily patinated with verdigris.

This type of effect is achieved by simply painting the surface of the object with a metallic bronze paint, prior to applying blue and green water-based glazes and ground-up chalk (whiting).

In the same way, new lead objects can be given the appearance of age by applying random patches of a dark gray-colored glaze and then allowing water to run over the surface to streak the paint and allow some of the base metal to show through. If you then repeat this process a few times using an off-white glaze, you will soon find that you have an authentic-looking painted patina effect.

Above: *This verdigris finish is courtesy of a sponging technique using ordinary artists' acrylic paints.*
Opposite: *Looking genuinely old, this chair has been treated with red oxide primer under the verdigris finish. To protect the surface from wear and weathering, two coats of a matte polyurethane varnish were applied.*

WOOD
EFFECTS

WOODGRAINING

The demand for woodgraining began in Europe during the early part of the 17th century. Initially confined to the homes of the wealthy, it was used to convert the appearance of inexpensive softwood wall paneling, doors, and dadoes into elaborately figured hardwoods, particularly in the so-called "lesser" rooms, or *salons*, where the use of hardwoods was deemed to be both unnecessary and overly expensive. By the middle of the 17th century woodgraining was regarded as a very highly skilled technique.

Left: *Fantasy woodgrained doors and paneling give a suitable period feel to the kitchen area of this house in England.*

59

In North America and Scandinavia there has been a long tradition of "folk art graining", in which itinerant craftsmen employed simple powder pigments in mediums such as beer, vinegar and even distemper to grain paneling, furniture and other domestic artifacts. Using materials as diverse as cork, oil-card, leather, leaves and even their fingers to manipulate the glazes, they produced bold, exuberant and highly decorative sketches that in many cases bore only a faint

resemblance to either the natural colour or the grain and figuring of any given wood.

Most hardwoods can be cut to reveal intricate and highly decorative graining and figuring. Consequently, many species, such as oak and walnut, have always been highly sought after for the construction of not only furniture, but also flooring, wall paneling, and doors. As a way of overcoming the expense of using such woods in quantity, especially in the less important rooms of a wealthy household, woodgraining was seen as an appropriate and cost-effective alternative. After priming the surface of the wood with two coats of a matte base-colored paint, you will need to prepare a

Above: *A paneled window shutter woodgrained in a light oak color.* **Opposite**: *The woodgraining on this well-traveled chest helps it to blend into a Texan period-bedroom setting.*

Above: *An imposingly large country kitchen dresser, woodgrained with an auburn mahogany finish, makes a magnificent showcase for vividly colored pottery.* **Opposite**: *This pair of inexpensive four-poster beds was made from plumber's piping disguised with a painted fantasy woodgrain effect.*

series of suitable colored glazes, using a transparent oil-based glaze as the basic medium mixed with different artists' pigments. An ordinary painter's brush is used to apply the background grain effect, while the detailed figurative work is applied using a small artist's paintbrush. You will need to study the pattern of the real wood in order to produce a realistic facsimile.

The initial response to the expense and scarcity of such hardwoods as maple and mahogany in the 17th century was an increasing use of veneers. Inevitably, however, the cost of producing good-quality veneers also became prohibitive and so craftsmen skilled in the techniques of woodgraining were called upon.

Unlike some other woodgraining techniques, both mahogany and maple woodgrain effects are best achieved using water-based, not oil-based, glazes. These produce a crisper, more authentic-looking finish, but the glazes do dry much faster. This means you must complete each stage of the process before moving quickly onto the next one. It is best to practise the more difficult aspects of the technique – such as bird's eye maple graining – on scrap wood first before committing yourself to the real wall paneling, door, or piece of furniture.

INDEX